COMPARING
ANIMAL TRAITS

GRIZZLY BEARS

HUGE HIBERNATING MAMMALS

REBECCA E. HIRSCH

Lerner Publications ◆ Minneapolis

Lerner Publications Company
A division of Lerner Publishing Group, Inc.
241 First Avenue North
Minneapolis, MN 55401 USA

For reading levels and more information, look up this title at www.lernerbooks.com.

Photo Acknowledgments

The images in this book are used with the permission of: © Dennis W. Donohue/Shutterstock.com, p. 1; © Galyna Andrushko/Shutterstock.com, p. 4; © Dawn Wilson Photo/Shutterstock.com, p. 5; © Dennis Donohue/Dreamstime.com, p. 6; © Laura Romin & Larry Dalton/Alamy, p. 7; © iStock/Thinkstock, p. 8; © Mark Payne-Gill/Nature Picture Library/Alamy, p. 10; © Paul Freed/Animals Animals, p. 11 (top); © Minden Pictures/SuperStock, p. 11 (bottom); © Mapping Specialists, Ltd., Madison, WI, p. 12; © Kelly Funk/Getty Images, p. 13; © Natalia Paklina/Buiten-beeld/Getty Images, p. 14; © Ingo Arndt/Getty Images, p. 15 (left); © Drew Buckley/Alamy, p. 15 (right); © John E Marriott/All Canada Photos/Getty Images, p. 16; © George Ostertag/Superstock/Alamy, p. 17 (left); US Fish and Wildlife Service, p. 17 (right); © Dennis W. Donohue/Shutterstock.com, p. 18; © Stouffer Productions/Animals Animals, p. 19; © Biosphoto/SuperStock, p. 20; © Rolf Nussbaumer/Alamy, p. 21 (top); http://www.birdphotos.com/Wikimedia Commons (CC BY 3.0), p. 21 (bottom); © J. L. "Woody" Wooden/Moment/Getty Images, p. 22; © Animals Animals/SuperStock, p. 23 (left); © Richard Wear/Design Pics Inc/Alamy, p. 23 (right); © iStockphoto.com/Dieter Meyrl, p. 24; © Daisy Gilardini/Oxford Scientific/Getty Images, p. 25; © Krzysztof Wiktor/Shutterstock.com, p. 26; © Animals Animals/SuperStock, p. 27 (left); © Gerard Lacz Images/SuperStock, p. 27 (right); © Meriel Lland/Oxford Scientific/Getty Images, p. 28; © John E Marriott/All Canada Photos/Getty Images, p. 29 (left); © Peter Macdiarmid/Getty Images, p. 29 (right).

Front cover: © iStockphoto.com/JudiLen.
Back cover: © Dennis Donohue/Dreamstime.com.

Main body text set in Calvert MT Std 12/18. Typeface provided by Monotype Typography.

Library of Congress Cataloging-in-Publication Data

Hirsch, Rebecca E., author.
    Grizzly bears : huge hibernating mammals / By Rebecca E. Hirsch.
        pages   cm. — (Comparing animal traits)
    Summary: "This book covers information (life cycle, appearance, habitat) about the grizzly bear. Each chapter discusses an aspect of the grizzly bear's life, comparing the bear to a similar mammal and to a very different mammal." —Provided by publisher.
    Audience: Ages 7–10.
    Includes bibliographical references and index.
    ISBN 978-1-4677-5578-8 (lib. bdg. : alk. paper) — ISBN 978-1-4677-6061-4 (pbk.) —
ISBN 978-1-4677-6217-5 (EB pdf)
    1. Grizzly bear—Juvenile literature. 2. Grizzly bear—Life cycles—Juvenile literature. I. Title.
QL737.C27H545 2015
599.784—dc23   2014027201

Manufactured in the United States of America
1 — BP — 12/31/14

TABLE OF CONTENTS

Introduction
MEET THE GRIZZLY BEAR 4

Chapter 1
WHAT DO GRIZZLY BEARS LOOK LIKE? 6

Chapter 2
WHERE GRIZZLY BEARS LIVE 12

Chapter 3
THE GRIZZLY BEAR'S YEAR 18

Chapter 4
THE LIFE CYCLE OF GRIZZLY BEARS 24

Grizzly Bear Trait Chart   30
Glossary   31
Selected Bibliography   32
Further Information   32
Index   32

MEET THE GRIZZLY BEAR

A grizzly bear stands in a roaring stream and plunges its head into the water. The bear comes up with a large silver fish in its mouth. Grizzly bears belong to a group of animals called mammals. Other groups of animals include insects, fish, amphibians, reptiles, and birds.

This grizzly bear has caught a fish! Grizzly bears eat both plants and animals.

What are mammals? Mammals are warm-blooded animals. This means they keep their bodies at a steady temperature. All mammals are vertebrates, or animals with backbones. All mammals have fur or hair. And all mammal mothers feed their babies milk. Grizzly bears share these traits with other mammals. But grizzly bears also have some traits that set them apart.

CHAPTER 1

WHAT DO GRIZZLY BEARS LOOK LIKE?

Grizzly bears are a member of the bear family. This family of mammals includes polar bears and giant pandas. A grizzly bear measures 3 to 4 feet (0.9 to 1.2 meters) at the shoulder and up to 8 feet (2.4 m) standing up. It weighs up to 800 pounds (363 kilograms). Male grizzly bears are almost twice as large as females.

The head of a grizzly bear is large and round. A grizzly bear has sharp teeth, round ears, and a muscular hump at its shoulders. It also has long claws on its front feet. The claws and the shoulder muscles make the grizzly a powerful digger.

DID YOU KNOW?

Grizzly bears are **BROWN BEARS** that live only in North America. Other brown bears live in Europe and Asia.

A grizzly bear is a kind of bear called a brown bear. Even so, a grizzly's fur may be blond, brown, or black. The thick fur covers the grizzly bear's head and body. Grizzly fur is often white-tipped, or grizzled, which is how the bear got its name.

GRIZZLY BEARS VS. WOLVERINES

Wolverines climb through snow-covered mountains and forests across northern Europe, Asia, and North America. Wolverines are the largest member of the weasel family. Although wolverines are much smaller than grizzly bears, the two animals look a lot alike. The Blackfoot American Indian term for wolverine even translates to "skunk bear."

Both grizzly bears and wolverines have rounded ears and pointy teeth. Wolverines can crush bone and chew through frozen meat with their powerful jaws. And like grizzly bears, wolverines have sharp claws. These claws help the wolverine dig and climb.

Some wolverines have pale stripes in their fur.

COMPARE IT!

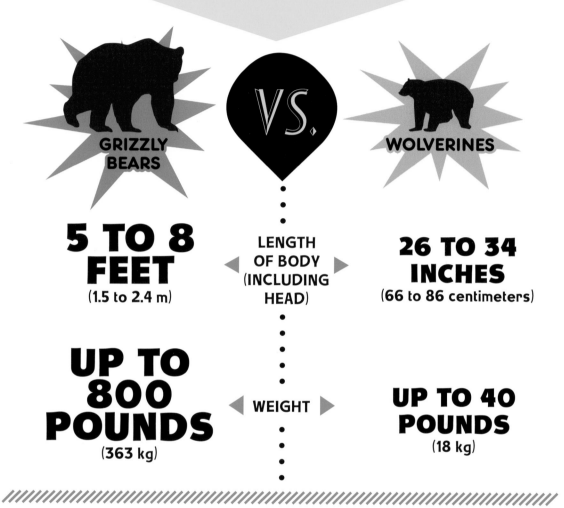

GRIZZLY BEARS VS. **WOLVERINES**

	LENGTH OF BODY (INCLUDING HEAD)	
5 TO 8 FEET (1.5 to 2.4 m)	◄ ►	**26 TO 34 INCHES** (66 to 86 centimeters)

	WEIGHT	
UP TO 800 POUNDS (363 kg)	◄ ►	**UP TO 40 POUNDS** (18 kg)

Both grizzly bears and wolverines have thick, shaggy fur. Wolverine fur can be dark brown or black. Light-colored stripes sometimes appear on the sides of a wolverine's body. Like the grizzly bear, the wolverine is built for cold weather. Its short legs and big feet are adapted for traveling across the snow.

GRIZZLY BEARS VS. THREE-BANDED ARMADILLOS

A three-banded armadillo pushes its snout into the dirt. The animal digs and sniffs for insects. Three-banded armadillos live in South America. These small mammals look very different from grizzly bears. Armadillos have tiny eyes and shovel-shaped snouts. Instead of the sharp teeth of grizzly bears, armadillos sport blunt teeth for crunching on insects.

A grizzly bear's body is furry. But an armadillo is nearly bald. Plates of armor cover the mammal's head, back, feet, and tail. The plates fit together like puzzle pieces, separated by leathery skin. When the armadillo feels threatened, it curls up into an armored ball.

Plates of armor fit together across an armadillo's body, protecting the animal from harm.

DID YOU KNOW?
An armadillo's armor is made of the same stuff as your fingernails. All armadillos have armor, but only three-banded armadillos can **CURL INTO A BALL.**

An armadillo does have hair, but the hair isn't thick like that of a grizzly bear. An armadillo has long, wiry hairs on its side and belly. As the armadillo moves around at night, the hairs brush against objects. The hairs help the armadillo feel its way in the dark.

An armadillo uses hairs on its side and belly to feel its way around.

CHAPTER 2

WHERE GRIZZLY BEARS LIVE

Grizzly bears can live in many habitats, **from thick forests to mountain meadows to Arctic** tundra. They can even live in desert habitats along rivers. Grizzlies once roamed across western North America. But people hunted the bears and destroyed their living spaces. In modern times, grizzly bears survive mostly in Alaska and Canada.

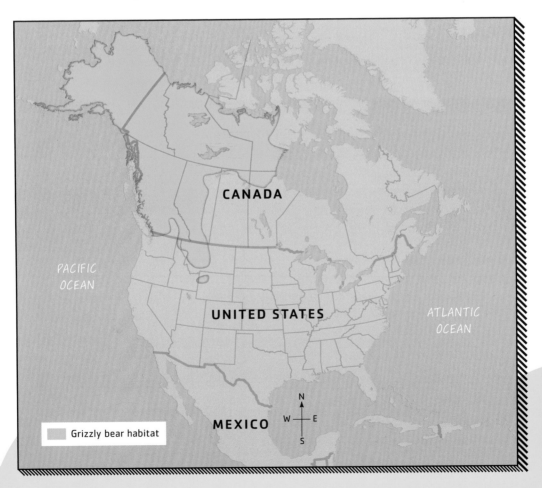

CANADA

PACIFIC
OCEAN

UNITED STATES

ATLANTIC
OCEAN

N
W — E
S

MEXICO

Grizzly bear habitat

These grizzly bears search for food in a forest. Their diet will change with the season and the food available.

Grizzly bears are omnivores, meaning they eat both plants and animals. They will even scavenge animal carcasses or dine on garbage. Their diet includes different foods during different seasons, depending on what is available nearby. Grizzly bears often fill up on nuts, berries, fruit, leaves, and roots. The bears can find these foods in spring, summer, and fall.

Grizzly bears eat animals when the bears can find and catch them. Grizzlies hunt insects, fish, ground squirrels, caribou, moose, elk, and farm animals. Some prey, such as spawning salmon, occupy grizzly habitats only at certain times of the year. But the broad diet of grizzlies helps the bears to stay full across the seasons.

GRIZZLY BEARS VS.
WILD BOARS

Wild boars roam across all continents except Antarctica. In the past, wild boars lived only in Europe, Asia, and northern Africa. But during the last few centuries, people brought wild boars to many places around the world. These settlers used boars as a source of food.

Wild boars live in both warm and cold climates.

Like grizzly bears, wild boars can survive in a range of habitats. Boars inhabit forests, grasslands, swamps, and farmland. Like grizzly bears, wild boars seek out places near water within these habitats. They also like to stay near trees. Trees help wild boars hide from predators. Grizzly bears don't mind snow and ice, but wild boars prefer to live where it is not too cold.

Like grizzlies, wild boars are not fussy about what they eat. They can find food throughout their many habitats. Wild boars will fill up on acorns, dig for roots with their tusks, or forage in farm fields. They will also eat worms, insects, slugs and snails, lizards, snakes, bird eggs, and rodents.

Both grizzly bears and wild boars are powerful diggers. Boars can destroy plants by digging. They may eat so much food that other animals can't find enough to eat.

GRIZZLY BEARS VS. BLACK-FOOTED FERRETS

A black-footed ferret scampers through the grass. It dives into a hole and disappears. These long, slender mammals live in the Great Plains of North America. Although black-footed ferrets and grizzly bears once lived in some of the same regions, their habitats are very different. Grizzly bears can live in many areas. Black-footed ferrets can survive only where prairie dog towns are found.

Unlike grizzly bears, black-footed ferrets are carnivores. Living near prairie dog towns (burrows) keeps the ferrets close to their main food source: prairie dogs. Prairie dog towns also give black-footed ferrets shelter. Inside the burrows, black-footed ferrets can hide from predators such as badgers and owls. At night, the ferrets go from burrow to burrow, hunting for prey.

Black-footed ferrets inhabit burrows on the plains of North America.

Black-footed ferrets' connection to prairie dogs has put the ferrets in danger. In the 1900s, farmers and ranchers killed huge numbers of prairie dogs to protect their fields. Many black-footed ferrets lost their habitat. Some people thought the ferrets were extinct. But in 1981, scientists discovered a small population in Wyoming. In recent years, scientists have brought black-footed ferrets back to many places.

COMPARE IT!

GRIZZLY BEARS

VS.

BLACK-FOOTED FERRETS

◀ HABITAT ▶

FORESTS, PRAIRIES, MOUNTAINS, TUNDRA, RIVER VALLEYS

PRAIRIE DOG TOWNS

◀ GEOGRAPHIC RANGE ▶

ALASKA AND WESTERN CANADA

SMALL AREAS OF THE WESTERN UNITED STATES AND MEXICO

◀ MAIN FOOD ▶

Nuts, berries, fruit, leaves, roots, insects, fish, small animals, caribou, moose, elk

Prairie dogs

CHAPTER 3

THE GRIZZLY BEAR'S YEAR

In summer and fall, grizzlies have big appetites. The huge bears need plenty of food to survive the long winter ahead. Grizzly bears feed in the early morning, eating as much as they can. They catch fish, stuff themselves on berries, and use their long claws to dig insects from rotting logs. Grizzly bears rest during the day. In the evening, grizzlies feed again. With all this feasting, a grizzly can gain 3 pounds (1 kg) a day!

Grizzly bears claw through logs to find insects to eat.

Grizzly bears spend most of the winter asleep in dens.

When winter comes, the fattened bear finds a hillside and digs a hole for its den. It may also move into a rock cave, a hollow tree, or a pile of brush. Inside the den, the animal falls into a deep sleep. Its heart rate and breathing slow. The grizzly does not eat or drink. Instead, it lives off its stored fat. This sleep is called hibernation. When spring comes, the hungry bear climbs out of its den and begins to eat again.

GRIZZLY BEARS VS. STRIPED SKUNKS

A striped skunk digs in a field at night. It feasts on a nest of turtle eggs. Striped skunks live across North America, in places with cold winters. These mammals survive the winter in ways similar to grizzly bears.

Both grizzly bears and skunks stuff themselves with food in summer and fall. Like grizzly bears, striped skunks are omnivores. These black-and-white mammals love fruit, nuts, and leaves. They also eat worms, insects, spiders, toads, frogs, lizards, snakes, mice, turtle eggs, and bird eggs. Skunks spend warm seasons raiding gardens, garbage cans, and bird feeders.

Striped skunks will scavenge garbage cans for food.

DID YOU KNOW?
Striped skunks are famous for their foul-smelling **SPRAY**. A skunk can spray an enemy from as far as 10 feet (3 m) away.

As winter nears, both grizzly bears and striped skunks put on thick layers of fat. The skunks waddle into their dens while the cold settles in. They fall into a deep winter sleep. Like grizzly bears, striped skunks can wake from time to time. Skunks may even come out on warm winter days to search for food. In spring, they leave their dens to forage once again.

Striped skunks hibernate in dens during the winter.

GRIZZLY BEARS VS. AMERICAN BISON

American bison graze the prairies of North America. These shaggy mammals are **herbivores**. They live in groups called herds. Bison live in some of the same places as grizzly bears—areas with cold winters. But they survive winter in different ways.

Grizzly bears spend winter inside a warm and sheltered den. But American bison remain active in the worst winter weather. Protected by thick fur and layers of fat, the members of a bison herd travel through snow in a line. The lead animal creates a path, and the herd follows. An animal that strays from the herd may find itself stranded in deep snow.

Inside their dens, grizzly bears go for months without eating. But bison spend winter looking for food. With their keen noses, they can sniff out grass under 3 feet (1 m) of snow. They swing their large heads to plow the snow away and then munch on the grasses underneath.

American bison travel
across the snow in a line.

COMPARE IT!

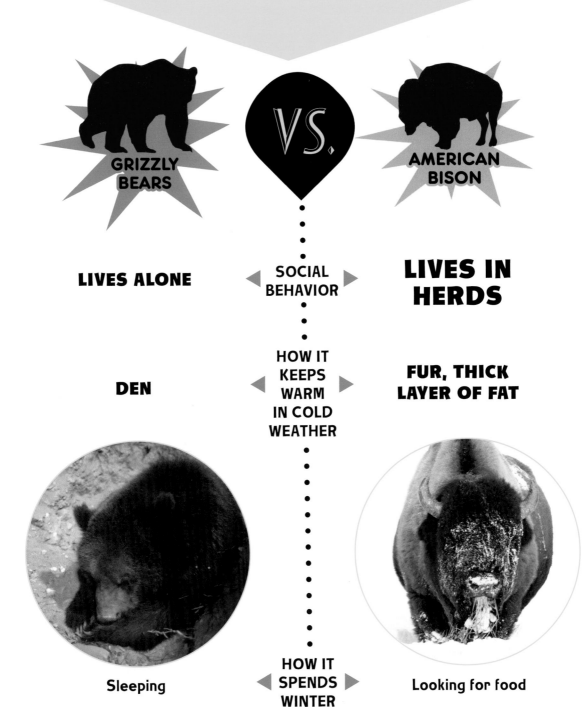

GRIZZLY BEARS

VS.

AMERICAN BISON

| LIVES ALONE | ◀ SOCIAL BEHAVIOR ▶ | **LIVES IN HERDS** |
| DEN | ◀ HOW IT KEEPS WARM IN COLD WEATHER ▶ | **FUR, THICK LAYER OF FAT** |

Sleeping

◀ HOW IT SPENDS WINTER ▶

Looking for food

CHAPTER 4

THE LIFE CYCLE OF GRIZZLY BEARS

The grizzly bear life cycle usually begins in the cold of winter. Inside the warm winter den, a female grizzly gives birth to one to three cubs. At first, grizzly cubs are blind and helpless. The cubs are also tiny compared to their mother.

Each grizzly cub weighs about 1 pound (0.5 kg) at birth. Fed on the mother's rich milk, a cub grows quickly. By spring, each cub weighs 10 to 20 pounds (4.5 to 9 kg). Then the cubs are ready to come out of the den.

DID YOU KNOW?
Male grizzly bears can harm **CUBS**, so mothers raise their cubs alone.

In warm seasons, the young cubs still depend on their mother to feed them and teach them how to find food. Later, they spend two to three more winters hibernating with their mother. After two or three years, the cubs are ready to live on their own. Grown grizzlies carry traits they have inherited from their parents. They have long claws, huge appetites, and the ability to hibernate. These traits help them survive for twenty to thirty years.

Grizzly bear cubs will stay close to their mother until they are fully grown.

GRIZZLY BEARS VS. JAGUARS

Jaguars stalk rain forests, grasslands, and deserts of South America. Jaguars and grizzly bears are solitary animals. Both of these mammals can survive in many habitats. The two mammals also share similar life cycles.

A female jaguar gives birth inside a cave or a canyon. She delivers one to four babies at a time. Like grizzly bear cubs, jaguar cubs cannot see at first. They depend on their mother for survival.

Jaguar cubs grow quickly on their mother's milk. By the time the cubs are two months old, they are ready to hunt with their mother. Jaguar mothers raise their young alone, as grizzly bear mothers do. The jaguar mother protects her cubs from other animals, including male jaguars.

Young jaguars are ready to hunt on their own at fifteen to eighteen months old. But they stay with their mother until they are two, about the same length of time that grizzly bears stay with their mothers. Then young jaguars leave to claim territories of their own. They can survive in the wild for up to twelve years.

Like grizzly cubs, young jaguars depend on their mother for food and protection.

GRIZZLY BEARS VS. TITI MONKEYS

Titi monkeys leap through the trees in the Amazon rain forest of South America. Titi monkeys live in families made up of their parents and their offspring. The furry monkeys dwell in different places than grizzly bears do. They have different life cycles too.

Female titi monkeys give birth to one baby at a time. Like all mammal mothers, the mother feeds her baby milk. But the father shares a stronger bond with the offspring. The titi monkey father carries the youngster on his back and brings the baby to its mother at nursing time.

The young titi monkey begins to eat solid food at three months old. The father gives it fruit, leaves, and insects. When the young monkey is four months old, it is able to find its own food. A titi monkey stays with its family for two or three years. Then it leaves. Unlike grizzly bears, titi monkeys don't live alone. A titi monkey finds a mate and starts a family of its own.

A baby titi monkey travels on the back of its father.

COMPARE IT!

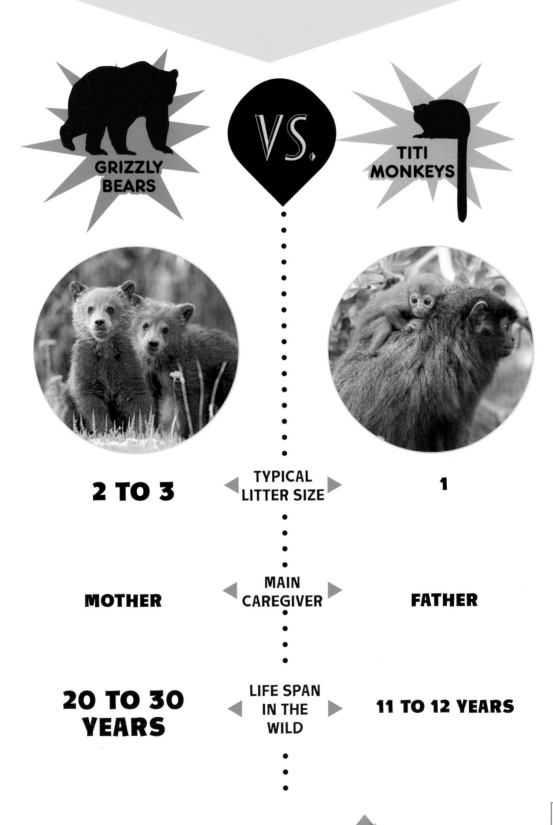

GRIZZLY BEARS

VS.

TITI MONKEYS

GRIZZLY BEARS		TITI MONKEYS
2 TO 3	TYPICAL LITTER SIZE	1
MOTHER	MAIN CAREGIVER	FATHER
20 TO 30 YEARS	LIFE SPAN IN THE WILD	11 TO 12 YEARS

GRIZZLY BEAR TRAIT CHART

This book explored grizzly bears and how they compare to other mammals. What other mammals would you like to learn about?

	WARM-BLOODED	HAIR ON BODY	GIVES BIRTH TO LIVE YOUNG	SHARP CLAWS	LIVES IN COLD HABITATS	HIBERNATES	
GRIZZLY BEAR	X	X	X	X	X	X	
WOLVERINE	X	X	X	X	X		
THREE-BANDED ARMADILLO	X	X	X	X			
WILD BOAR	X	X	X		X		
BLACK-FOOTED FERRET	X	X	X	X	X		
STRIPED SKUNK	X	X	X	X	X	X	
AMERICAN BISON	X	X	X		X		
JAGUAR	X	X	X	X			
TITI MONKEY	X	X	X				

GLOSSARY

adapted: suited to living in a particular environment

carnivores: meat-eating animals

extinct: no longer existing

forage: to search an area for food

habitats: environments where an animal naturally lives. A habitat is the place where an animal can find food, water, air, shelter, and a place to raise its young.

herbivores: plant-eating animals

hibernation: the state of spending winter at rest

omnivores: animals that eat both plants and meat

predators: animals that hunt, or prey on, other animals

prey: an animal that is hunted and killed by a predator for food

scavenge: to eat food that has been discarded, such as the remains of prey killed by other animals

solitary: living by itself. Solitary animals spend most of their time alone, except for mating and raising young.

spawning: mating

territories: areas of land that are occupied and defended by an animal

traits: features that are inherited from parents. Body size and fur color are examples of inherited traits.

tundra: a cold, treeless Arctic plain with a permanently frozen layer below the ground

ELECTED BIBLIOGRAPHY

asic Facts about Grizzly Bears."
fenders of Wildlife. June 24, 2014.
p://www.defenders.org/grizzly-bear
asic-facts.

wey, Tanya, and Liz Ballenger. "*Ursus
ctos* (Brown Bear)." Animal Diversity
eb. July 6, 2014. http://animaldiversity
nmz.umich.edu/accounts/Ursus_arctos/.

rizzly Bear." National Wildlife
undation. June 24, 2014. http://
vw.nwf.org/wildlife/wildlife-library
ammals/grizzly-bear.aspx.

"Grizzly Bear (*Ursus arctos horribilis*)." US
Fish and Wildlife. June 24, 2014. http://
www.fws.gov/mountain-prairie/species
/mammals/grizzly/grizzly_bear.pdf.

"Grizzly Bear: *Ursus arctos horribilis*."
National Geographic. June 24, 2014.
http://animals.nationalgeographic.com
/animals/mammals/grizzly-bear/.

Macdonald, David. *The Encyclopedia of
Mammals*. Vol. 2. New York: Facts on File,
2001.

URTHER INFORMATION

nosky, Jim. *Tooth and Claw: The
ld World of Big Predators*. New York:
erling Children's Books, 2014. Pick up
s book to learn more about the lives of
d mammal predators.

vironmental Education for Kids—Snug
he Snow
p://dnr.wi.gov/org/caer/ce/eek
ature/snugsnow.htm
this page from the Wisconsin
partment of Natural Resources,
itors can learn about how different
mals hibernate.

rkle, Sandra. *Grizzly Bears*.
nneapolis: Lerner Publications, 2010.
s book by science writer Sandra

Markle features stunning photographs of
grizzly bears in their natural habitats.

National Wildlife Federation—Grizzly Bear
http://www.nwf.org/Wildlife/Wildlife
-Library/Mammals/Grizzly-Bear.aspx
This page from the National Wildlife
Federation site has fun facts about the
grizzly bear, as well as information about
the ways people protect grizzly bear
habitats.

San Diego Zoo—Mammals: Brown Bear
http://animals.sandiegozoo.org/animals
/brown-bear
Visit this site for more details about the
lives of grizzly bears, and watch a video
of a grizzly at mealtime.

IDEX

zzly bear comparisons:
s. American bison,
2–23; vs. black-
ooted ferrets, 16–17;
s. jaguars, 26–27;
s. striped skunks,
0–21; vs. three-banded
rmadillos, 10–11; vs.

titi monkeys, 28–29; vs.
wild boars, 14–15; vs.
wolverines, 8–9
grizzly bears: diet, 13;
habitat, 12; life cycle,
24–25; size, 6, 9; traits,
6–7

hibernation, 19, 21, 25

mammal features, 5

trait chart, 30
types of habitats: deserts,
12, 26; forests, 8, 12, 15,
17; mountains, 8, 12, 17;
plains, 16; prairies, 17,
22; rain forests, 26, 28;
tundra, 12, 17